# A CHRISTMAS CAROL

# A CHRISTMAS CAROL

**Adapted by Stephen Sharkey**
**Based on the novel by Charles Dickens**

## JOSEF WEINBERGER PLAYS

LONDON

A CHRISTMAS CAROL
First published in 2010
by Josef Weinberger Ltd
12-14 Mortimer Street, London, W1T 3JJ
www.josef-weinberger.com
general.info@jwmail.co.uk

ISBN    978 0 85676 321 2

Printed in England by Good News Press Ltd, Ongar, Essex

A CHRISTMAS CAROL was first produced by Northern Stage, Newcastle on November 24th 2007. The cast was as follows:

| | |
|---|---|
| GHOST OF CHRISTMAS PRESENT/MR KING | Rod Arthur |
| ELIZABETH/MARTHA/FAN | Helen Buchanan |
| BELLE/BETTY/BELINDA | Susie Burton |
| BOB CRATCHIT/LAMBERT/TOPPER/RICHARD | Mark Calvert |
| EBENEZER SCROOGE | Michael Hodgson |
| MARLEY/SCROOGE'S FATHER/MR FEZZIWIG/ ALF/MR FALKNER | Donald McBride |
| SAIREY/SCHROOGE'S MOTHER/LUCY | Carol McGuigan |
| MRS CRATCHIT/MRS FEZZIWIG/ MISS LEMON | Josephine Myddleton |
| FRED/YOUNG SCROOGE/EBENEZER/PETER | Christopher Price |
| TIM/FAGIN | Scott Turnbull |

CHORUS

Simon Alexander Cairns
James Crowther
Adele Evitt
Jessica Johnson
Judy Natasha Carr
Bill Pickard
David Robson
Tori Sunners

Directed by Erica Whyman
Designed by Neil Murray
Lighting design by Charles Balfour
Original music by Olly Fox
Choreography by Nick Whitehouse
Sound Design by Rob Brown

Street chorus

Mat
Luke
leyral
Johnny
Murphy
James
Roger or Aidan
Ruth

litt Me

↑ dark
L.

Avoid
Personal
Pronouns!

The / before o vowel
Vowel
Thee

prois
up
Ques.

Scene 1

The Theatre comes to London

## ACT ONE

## STAVE ONE

*After a raucous rendition of one of the more hedonistic Christmas carols, the stage is suddenly quiet and dark.* CHARLES DICKENS *enters.*

DICKENS

My good friends! Hello. Compliments of the season, and a warm welcome to each and every one of you this winter's morn (afternoon / eve.) You are about to see a ghost story. It is the humble hope and wish of the company that by the showing of it, our little play will raise the ghost of an idea. The idea of Christmas. And tonight, when you lay your head on the pillow to sleep, may it haunt your dreams pleasantly, and make you smile to think of us.

(DICKENS *becomes* EBENEZER SCROOGE *before our eyes.*)

CHORUS

Ebenezer Scrooge
The meanest man in England
His heart is frozen solid in his chest
The cold within him's catching
His icy eyes
Freeze you with a look
No warmth can warm
Nor wintry weather chill him
Nobody ever stops him in the street to say
My dear Scrooge!
How the devil are you?
Come to dinner this evening!
Men women and children
Cross the street to avoid him
Which is fine by him
The way he likes it
He's secretive
Self-contained
Solitary as an oyster in his shell.

(SCROOGE *takes his place in his Counting House, opposite the humbler station of* BOB,

*who is working feverishly to finish his work
before closing.*)

CHORUS        Here he is, that Christmas Eve
              A businessman
              Business as usual
              Little suspecting
              Never imagining
              His whole world
              His whole life
              Is About To Be Turned Upside Down
              Inside Out
              And Back To Front

SCROOGE       Cratchit.

BOB           Yes, Mister Scrooge, sir.

SCROOGE       Did you put a coal on the fire while I was at
              luncheon?

BOB           No, sir.

SCROOGE       You are quite certain of that?

BOB           I am, sir.

SCROOGE       Hmmm.

CHORUS        Scrooge is in his counting house . . .

SCROOGE       If you wish to be warmer . . .

CHORUS        And his clerk, Bob Cratchit . . .

SCROOGE       I suggest . . .

CHORUS        Is counting all his money.

SCROOGE       You tell your wife – you do have a wife, don't
              you?

BOB           I do, sir.

| | |
|---|---|
| SCROOGE | Tell her to knit you a thicker scarf. |

| | |
|---|---|
| CHORUS | What does he care |

Song 3

About Christmas Eve?
There are profits to be made
Debts to call in
Borrowers to squeeze
In his grasping / clutching / unforgiving fist.
No time to spare
Time is money
No time for the niceties
The kindness of strangers
The ties that bind us to each other

(FRED *has entered and exclaims . . .* )

| | |
|---|---|
| FRED | A Merry Christmas, Uncle! God keep you! |

(SCROOGE *turns and fixes his nephew with an icy stare.*)

| | |
|---|---|
| CHORUS | His nephew Fred |

His dead sister's boy
His only living relative
Every single Christmas Eve — me
Fred comes by
To wish his Uncle Ebenezer
Happiness — sab
And every single Christmas Eve — me
The same — me
Hard
Cold
Shoulder            — Shot 2 came down
                       from the Bridge

| | |
|---|---|
| SCROOGE | BAAAHH! |
| FRED | Oh, Uncle, you really . . . |
| SCROOGE | BAAAHH! I say. It's all humbug. |
| FRED | You don't mean that, I'm sure . . . |

SCROOGE    Oh you're sure, are you? Merry Christmas? What reason have you to be merry? You're poor enough.

FRED    What reason then have you to be so gloomy? You're *rich* enough.

SCROOGE and CHORUS    BAAAHH!!

SCROOGE    Humbug.

FRED    Don't be cross with me, uncle . . .

SCROOGE    What's Christmas to you? You're a year older, and not a penny richer, that's all. If I had my will, every idiot who goes about with Merry Christmas on his lips would be boiled with his own pudding, and buried with a stake of holly through his heart. So . . .

SCROOGE and CHORUS    BAAAHH!!

FRED    I am sure –

SCROOGE    Again with his 'I am sure'!

FRED    (*refusing to be ruffled*) I am sure that Christmas is a kind, forgiving time, when we think of people less fortunate than us as if – as if they really *are* fellow travellers through life, and not – not some wildly different species. I believe it *does* do me good to celebrate Christmas, and so I say, God bless it!

(BOB *applauds, then stops of a sudden, aware of* SCROOGE'S *wrathful gaze upon him.*)

CHORUS    Oh dear.
Bob has a wife
And four children
The last thing he needs
On Christmas Eve
Is the sack

(SCROOGE, *turning to* FRED.)

*argument*

SCROOGE
You are quite a powerful speaker, sir. You should stand for Parliament.

FRED
Don't be angry, Uncle. Won't you come to Christmas dinner at our house. My wife and my friends would be delighted –

SCROOGE
(*interrupting*) Would they now. Christmas dinner, you say.

FRED
(*seeing a glimmer, he thinks*) Oh do come – Betty will be so pleased – there's to be a goose, and a turkey, and afterwards we shall have *such* a game . . .

SCROOGE
Why did you marry?

FRED
Why – why did I marry . . . ? Uncle. Really.

SCROOGE
The reason, if you please.

FRED
Because I fell in love with Betty, of course, why else . . .

*pathetic*

SCROOGE
(*mocking*) Because you fell in love! Oh dear. (*Grimly serious again.*) It will be a cold day in Hell before you see me at your table.

FRED
Uncle – please . . .

SCROOGE
Good afternoon.

FRED
Why can we not be friends?

SCROOGE
Good afternoon.

FRED
Uncle, I am sorry with all my heart that you refuse to be a part of my life. I know you loved my mother very much when you were children, she often told me so . . .

SCROOGE
Good afternoon.

FRED            I cannot, *will* not be angry with you, for her
                sake. So fare you well, brother of my mother –
                and a Merry Christmas!

SCROOGE         Good afternoon!

                (FRED *turns to go,* BOB *leaps up to see him out.
                They wish each other Merry Christmas at the
                door.* SCROOGE *sees this and picks up a stick or
                ruler or poker and brings it crashing down on*
                BOB's *desk, and he scurries back. As* FRED
                *exits he is almost bowled over by* MISS LEMON.)

FRED            And a Happy New Year!

                (*And* FRED *is finally gone. Awkward silence,
                then* . . . )

SCROOGE         Who are you and what do you want.

MISS LEMON      Ah, yes – my good sir – you will forgive my
                calling on you at this busy time . . .

SCROOGE         Will I. Your name.

MISS LEMON      Umm – Miss Lemon, at your service . . .

SCROOGE         Lemon, ey. Will I slice you or grate you.

                (MISS LEMON *laughs, terrified.*)

                What's your business, Lemon? Quick about it.

MISS LEMON      (*consulting her papers*) Ummm . . . Now. Oh.
                Have I the pleasure of addressing Mr Scrooge,
                or Mr Marley?

SCROOGE         (*going up to* MISS LEMON) State your business.

MISS LEMON      At this festive season, Mr Marley – It is our
                duty to make some slight provision for the
                poor and the homeless, who suffer greatly . . .

SCROOGE         Marley's dead.

MISS LEMON     Oh. Oh dear.

SCROOGE     Dead as a doornail.

MISS LEMON     Exceedingly sorry to hear it – my sincerest
condolences . . .

SCROOGE     (*cutting her off*) Seven years ago he died.
Seven years this very night.

        (*A shiver passes through the room.* MISS
LEMON *is spooked.*)

MISS LEMON     No doubt his generosity is well represented by
his surviving partner . . .

CHORUS     No doubt.
The late Jacob Marley
Was just as mean
And hard-hearted
As his 'surviving partner'.

MISS LEMON     When so many thousands lack the common
comforts, which you and I take for granted . . .

SCROOGE     Are there no prisons?

MISS LEMON     Plenty of prisons, yes indeed . . .

SCROOGE     And the workhouses? The treadmills?

MISS LEMON     Oh, very busy, sir . . .

SCROOGE     Good, good, I am glad. I was afraid something
had occurred to stop them in their useful
course.

MISS LEMON     (*is confused but soldiers on . . .* ) A few of us
in the City are raising a fund to buy the poor
some meat and drink, and means of warmth.
How much shall we put you down for, Mr
Scrooge?

SCROOGE     Put me down for – nothing.

MISS LEMON    You wish to be anonymous?

SCROOGE       I wish to be left alone. I don't make merry at
              Christmas and I can't afford to make idle
              people merry. Let them go to the workhouses
              and the rest – I help to support them and they
              cost quite enough.

MISS LEMON    But – many would rather die than go to such
              dreadful places . . .

SCROOGE       (*explodes*) THEN THEY HAD BETTER DIE!

              (MISS LEMON *stands petrified.*)

                          *Let them*

SCROOGE       They had better die, I say, and decrease the
              surplus population. I bid you a very good
              afternoon, madam. Now GET OUT!

              (MISS LEMON *flees in terror, but of course as
              she does so she can't help but says* . . . )

MISS LEMON    Merry Christmas!

CHORUS        Scrooge resumes his labours
              With an improved opinion of himself.
              Outside
              The frosty, foggy air
              Begins to bite  – *Lenvil*
          *Me* – As the homeless boy
              The one who sweeps the street for pennies
              Comes a-carolling

JOHN THE
CROSSING
SWEEPER       (*sings*) We three Kings of Orient are
              Bearing gifts we traverse afar
              Field and fountain, moor and mountain –

              (SCROOGE *is near the door and slams it shut on
              him, he cries out in pain.*)

CHORUS        Cratchit  – *Me*
              His bony fingers

Numb with cold
Scratches at the ledger
His eyes are swimming
In shillings and pence
His mind is drifting
His heart isn't in it
Its four miles hence
With his dear wife
His children
Peter
Martha
Belinda
And poor little Timothy

(*The bell tolls three, and* BOB *closes his book and gets ready to leave, it's home time.*)

SCROOGE        You want the whole of tomorrow off I suppose.

BOB        If quite convenient, sir.

SCROOGE        No, it is not convenient. A day's pay for no work? A poor excuse for picking a man's pocket every twenty-fifth of December. Be here all the earlier next morning.

BOB        Yes sir, Mr Scrooge.

SCROOGE        Go then.

CHORUS        And that's that
Bob's away
Like lightning
Laughing and leaping
The whole way to Baynham Street
Pausing only
At an ice slide by St Paul's

BOB        Goodness, that looks fun . . .

CHORUS        And down he goes
Whizzing down
Twenty times or more

In honour of Christmas Eve
And the lightness and the brightness
Burning in his large heart

**BOB**      WHOOO HOOO!!

**CHORUS**      Meanwhile.
Scrooge takes his usual grim supper
In the usual grim tavern –
Cabbage soup,
Pig's trotters in jelly
Then takes himself home
To bed.
Bed.
BED.
Our favourite place
Our hope and comfort
Where we dream
And forget
And refresh ourselves.
The house is buried away
In a dark yard
Where no house ought to be.
When it was little
It was playing hide and seek
With all the other little houses
Hid itself here
And forgot the way out.
Now it's old and broken
Gloomy as the grave
Lonely and unloved

(SCROOGE *approaches the front door, groping
in the dark.*)

It once belonged
To Jacob Marley.

(SCROOGE *takes out his key.*)

Who is
Who has been
Remember
Dead as a doornail

These seven years
Dead
Indeed
As a door knocker . . .

*(The face of* JACOB MARLEY *looms out of the gloom. Quite calm, with his spectacles pushed back up on his forehead.* SCROOGE *drops his keys.)*

SCROOGE        Jacob?

*(Just as suddenly as it appeared, the face retreats into the gloom.* SCROOGE *begins to recover himself, picks up his keys.)*

CHORUS         Scrooge had not missed him
               Dreamed of him
               Hardly mentioned his name
               Until today
               Tonight
               Here and now
               He's terrified
               The dead man is with him . . .

*(*SCROOGE *lights a candle, and surveys the room. Satisfied he is alone he puts on his dressing-gown, slippers and night-cap and seats himself by the very small fire. A tinkly little bell rings. Then another. Then a third, a handbell. And so on up the range, each noisier and heavier than the last until a deep, deep CLONG from the solemnest church bell, the bell that tolls for HIM.)*

SCROOGE        It's all humbug! I won't believe it. I won't!

*(The fire in the grate roars up,* SCROOGE *cries out in fear.)*

               It's humbug, I say! Nonsense!

*(The CLANK and SCRANK of chains, heavy iron links, being dragged along . . .)*

Twaddle! Gubbins! Piffle! Rubbish!

(MARLEY'S GHOST *enters. "The chain he drew was clasped about his middle. It was long, and wound about him like a tail; and it was made (for* SCROOGE *observed it closely) of cash-boxes, keys, padlocks, ledgers, deeds, and heavy purses wrought in steel."* )

It cannot be – ! What are you – ?

MARLEY      You know me.

SCROOGE     His voice! What do you want?

MARLEY      Much.

SCROOGE     Not there. You are not there, I say!

MARLEY      And yet – you see me.

SCROOGE     I might be ill, or – or it's indigestion – you could be a blot of mustard, a crumb of cheese –

(MARLEY'S GHOST *raises a terrible cry, and shakes its chains.* SCROOGE *is terrified.*)

MARLEY      This is the chain I forged in life. Your own is just as full and heavy, mark my words –

SCROOGE     My own? I don't see it –

MARLEY      And yet you wear it. I am here to tell you. To warn you.

SCROOGE     Warn me?

MARLEY      I led a bitter, selfish life, mastered by greed. Now in death I wander the earth, to witness everywhere the happiness I never shared – oh Woe! Woe for my wasted heart!

SCROOGE     You were a good man of business, Jacob –

MARLEY
MANKIND should have been my business! I suffer most at Christmastime. I walk through the holiday crowds, longing for a kind word, a smile – but I am invisible!

(MARLEY'S GHOST *raises another terrible, pitiful cry,* SCROOGE *shrinks from it.*)

This will be YOUR fate. FOREVER, Ebenezer.

SCROOGE
Oh mercy!

MARLEY
You have a chance to escape it –

SCROOGE
Tell me how!

MARLEY
You will be haunted.

SCROOGE
More ghosts?

MARLEY
Three Spirits will come to you. Expect the first tomorrow, when the bell tolls One . . . the Second on the next night, at the same hour –

SCROOGE
Couldn't I take 'em all at once and get it over with??

MARLEY
The Third the next night on the last stroke of Twelve. Without their help, you will suffer as I do, and worse. My time is gone. Remember me!

(*"The apparition walked backward from him; and, at every step it took, the window raised itself a little, so that, when the spectre reached it, it was wide open. It beckoned Scrooge to approach, which he did. When they were within two paces of each other, Marley's Ghost held up its hand, warning him to come no nearer. Scrooge stopped . . . became sensible of confused noises in the air; incoherent sounds of lamentation and regret; wailings inexpressibly sorrowful and self-*

*accusatory. The spectre, after listening for a*
*moment, joined in the mournful dirge; and*
*floated out upon the dark, bleak night."*)

SCROOGE          H –
                 H –
                 Hu –
                 Hu –
                 Hum –
                 Humb –

(SCROOGE *staggers to bed, and lies down in a*
*stupor. The* CHORUS *tuck him in.*)

Scene 5

## STAVE TWO
### The First Of The Three Spirits

In bed not quite asleep.

CHORUS           Fast asleep
                 A sleep so deep
                 That any soul                    Song 7
                 That came within
                 Might have said
                 He was dead –

(SCROOGE *wakes with a start, as a bell strikes*
*the four quarters.*)

SCROOGE          (*listening*) Still dark . . . What's the hour?

CHORUS           (*counts as the bell tolls the hour*)
                 One o' clock . . .

                 (*All the way to . . .*)          The crys of London

SCROOGE          Twelve o'clock! I can't have slept the whole
                 day, into the next night? Could it be noon, and
                 the sun forgot to rise?? I remember I dreamed
                 – I dreamed I saw old Jacob, a phantom, bound
                 in chains – BAAAHH. It's all –

                 (*The clock strikes the quarter hour.* SCROOGE
                 *stops to listen.*)

Hey, that was quick –

(*The clock strikes the half hour.*)

Quicker yet – I am still dreaming!

(*The clock strikes the third quarter.*)

One o'clock is next – the hour he said I would be visited – by a Spirit! Oh!

(*The clock strikes one. The room fills with a brilliant white light, and the noise of the city at work – the horns on the river barges, the shouts of street traders, the horses and carriages thundering by.* SCROOGE *is stunned, and cowers as the noise gets louder . . .And stops. And the light with it – the only light is that shed by a lantern . . .*)

(*Standing by his bed is* FAGIN, *a boy* SCROOGE *once knew when they worked together at a factory by the river, putting labels on bottles of boot blacking.* SCROOGE *was twelve years old at the time,* FAGIN *three years older. He wears a ragged apron, ill-fitting cap, hob-nailed boots, the whole lot dirty and stained. He carries a lantern on a pole.*)

SCROOGE   Who are you? What are you?

FAGIN   I am the Ghost of Christmas Past.

SCROOGE   Long past?

FAGIN   No. Your past. Look at me.

SCROOGE   I am looking.

FAGIN   Apron. Lantern. Oil stains all over.

SCROOGE   Good Heaven!

FAGIN   I used to light the lamps at dusk.

*[handwritten: Specter of an old friend   scene 6]*

SCROOGE        Fagin! Is it? Jimmy Fagin, as I live!

FAGIN          The same. How d'you do, Young Gentleman –

               (CHORUS *bring on the frame of a full length
               mirror.*)

SCROOGE        That's what you called me, you and the other
               boys in the factory . . . What is this – ?

FAGIN          (*approaches*) Don't be afraid. Look in the
               mirror. What do you see?

               (SCROOGE *walks over and looks into the mirror.*)

SCROOGE        It's . . . it's me . . .

FAGIN          You're twelve years old. What're you doing?

SCROOGE        Working. In Lamberts factory

FAGIN          In Lambert's factory by the river. Ten hours a
               day, five days a week. Take your pot of boot
               black, cover with oil-paper –

SCROOGE        Paste it on. Then the same with the blue paper –

FAGIN          Then tie it round with string –

SCROOGE        Then clip the paper so's it's close and neat all
               round –

FAGIN          What time's dinner?

SCROOGE        Twelve o'clock.

FAGIN          What time's tea?

SCROOGE        Half past three.

FAGIN          What time's your mother and father coming to
               take you home for Christmas? You're
               trembling, Young Gentleman.

| SCROOGE | I don't wish to remember. |
|---|---|
| FAGIN | Tough. |
| SCROOGE | Have you come to torment me? |
| FAGIN | No. To light the dark, Young Gentleman. Walk through. |
| SCROOGE | Walk through – ? |
| FAGIN | To see the shadows of the things that made you who you are. |

*Scene 7*

|  | (*They pass through the mirror, and into the Blacking Factory. There are a group of boys seated in a semi-circle, and the* YOUNG SCROOGE *is reading to them.*) *into the black factory of the pass* |
|---|---|
| FAGIN | It is Christmas Eve, forty winters past. |
| SCROOGE | The boys! Hey – Bucktooth! Frankie! It's me – it's Ebenezer – ! |
| FAGIN | They can't hear you. Lost in the time past. And the story of Ali Baba – |
| SCROOGE | I used to love to tell stories. |
| FAGIN | You saw the characters alive when you read, your imagination was so fierce back then, wannit, Young Gentleman. |
| YOUNG SCROOGE | (*reading*) Kasim cried out in an excited voice – OPEN SESAME! And the door in the rock opened wide. Kasim entered the cave, gawping at the gold and diamonds and money lying everywhere. The door shut behind him. But he didn't bother about that. Giddy with greed and excitement, he filled six large sacks with treasure. But when he was ready to leave, he realised he had forgotten the magic words. He |

tried OPEN, BARLEY! And OPEN, MILLET!,
and as many kinds of seed as he could
remember, but none worked. He was trapped . . .

(YOUNG SCROOGE *continues to read, but we
can't hear him, it's as if the sound has been
turned off.*)

FAGIN        You were the only one as could read and write.
You'd been to school, grew up in a nice house.
But your father fell to gambling, drowned in
debt, and the seven and six you could bring in
was very needed . . .

(*A* BOY *who has been posted sentry comes
running in and shouts.*)

BOY          Lambert!

(*And all the boys scramble onto benches to
resume their work. As they do so they start up
a rendition of 'God Rest Ye Merry Gentlemen'.*
MR LAMBERT *enters, ushering in* SCROOGE'S
MOTHER, FATHER *and* SISTER.)

LAMBERT      That's it boys! Very festive, very festive
indeed, do you not think so, Mister Scrooge?,
Mrs Scrooge? The boys are ever cheery at
their work, your eldest ever in the front rank in
that regard, ey Ebenezer? And none of his old
trouble lately, very pleased indeed I am to tell
you that.

FAGIN        The old trouble.

SCROOGE      My fits – I used to have fits when I was
anxious and melancholy –

LAMBERT      Come out boy, here is your father and your
mother –

(ELIZABETH *runs to her brother and they hold
each other tightly.*)

And dear Lizzie, of course, your sister – well that is charming in the ultimate –

ELIZABETH    (*snapping at him*) My name is Elizabeth, I'll have you know, sir.

MRS SCROOGE    Please you Mr Lambert, she is always very particular about it.

LAMBERT    As she was christened Elizabeth at the font, so shall we honour each and every delightful vowel and consonant, every syllable shall be of equal –

MR SCROOGE    Mr Lambert.

MRS SCROOGE    We had better not – put the matter off.

LAMBERT    Ah no, indeed.

ELIZABETH    But – you're not going to tell him here, are you? Father, no –

MR SCROOGE    Ebenezer, my dear son –

YOUNG
SCROOGE    What's going on – ?

MR SCROOGE    It is very difficult to say the words, I hardly know where I should begin –

MRS SCROOGE    (*interrupting*) For God's sake.

MR SCROOGE    I am bankrupt, Ebenezer. I must go to the debtors' prison –

YOUNG
SCROOGE    Prison!

MR SCROOGE    – and your mother and sister will stay there with me.

YOUNG
SCROOGE    What about me? Am I to come, too? What about me?

(*The* SCROOGES *melt away, and* LAMBERT, *and the* FACTORY BOYS.)

*Scene 8  The poor boy scrooge* [handwritten]

FAGIN
Aye, what about you. Lambert got you this room in a lodging house, and the next two and a half years you'll trudge back and forth to the factory, all for your seven and six. And here you are, Christmas eve, lonely as the Moon, unwrapping a tiny packet of cheese and bread for your supper, as the bells ring out for Christmas Day –

(YOUNG SCROOGE *puts some food in his mouth, and immediately starts to cry . . .*)

SCROOGE
Poor boy!

(FAGIN *goes and gently turns down the light by the poor boy's bed.*)

FAGIN
Let us away now. What is it, Young Gentleman?

SCROOGE
John the homeless boy. He came to my door to sing a Christmas carol –

FAGIN
What of it?

SCROOGE
I might have given him something, that's all –

FAGIN
We're away.

SCROOGE
Away where – ?

FAGIN
To another of your Christmases past.

*Scene 9* [handwritten]

*The Perriwinkle* [handwritten]

(FAGIN *and his lamp lead* SCROOGE *to another scene.*)

You know what Christmas is to people. What it can be. Look here. Do you know this fella, do you think?

(*A large man in a wig is discovered behind a desk.* SCROOGE *is beside himself.*)

SCROOGE    It's old Fezziwig! Bless his heart! It's Fezziwig, alive again!

(*The impressive figure stands and extracts his pocket watch from his waistcoat, consults it, and gives the chain a swing or two before returning it to the pocket.*)

FEZZIWIG    BOYS! LET'S HAVE YOU, BOYS!

SCROOGE    I was apprenticed ~~here, in this warehouse~~ to this men... Fezziwig taught me everything, how to keep the books, draw up accounts –

FAGIN    And how to keep Christmas, ey?

FEZZIWIG    CHARLEY! EBENEZER! SEVEN OF THE CLOCK!

(*The apprentices come running in, carrying books and papers.*)

Books away, boys! Away with them! No more work today you silly men, it's Christmas Eve! Away with these at the double – hip ho! We'll need every inch, let's see how fast we can blast ourselves a ballroom! Hilli-ho Charley! That's it! Ebenezer – come here man!

(EBENEZER *comes.*)

What *do* you look like, sir. What sort of toastmaster goes about in muddy green and grey?

(FEZZIWIG *produces a very bright and gaudy waistcoat and tie.*)

A present for you. Did you ever see a dull flower? No. Why? The colour they use to attract the bees. Get yourself noticed, laddy. Hide not your light.

(*He helps* EBENEZER *get changed.*)

FAGIN            Do you hear that?

SCROOGE          I do.

FEZZIWIG         You enjoy yourself, son. You've worked hard for me this year. I thank you for it. Charley! You may tell my good lady, we are ready to receive her! And all her distinguished guests!

                 (*Music.* MRS FEZZIWIG *and her entourage appear, bringing in plates and trolleys and all manner of receptacles overflowing with goodies.*)

MRS FEZZIWIG     Come one, come all!! Let's have them in!!

                 (*Music, and in come the Revellers, each handing their invitation to* EBENEZER *to announce them.*)

YOUNG
SCROOGE          Mr Tom Fielding, from over the way! Mrs Jane Humbleton and Miss Ella Humbleton, from Number 45! Mr Bernard Lester and Mrs Lizzie Lester, from Tipping Lane! Mr Thomas Goodbody and Miss Brenda Grayson, best friends of the Fezziwigs! Mr Peter Fairlie and Miss Polly Fairlie of Fairlie and Fairlie!

                 (*And so on. There is soon enough a very jolly gathering, and cake and drink is consumed, and glasses clinked, and bows and curtseys made . . .* )

MRS FEZZIWIG     Ladies and Gentlemen, boys and girls, it gives me the greatest pleasure to declare the annual Fezziwig Christmas Ball . . . is begun!

(*And away they go with their formal dances, to the delight of* SCROOGE *who claps and stamps his feet and gets quite carried away, mirroring the excitement of his younger self. When the party breaks up and reconvenes for another pass,* MRS FEZZIWIG *calls out.*)

MRS FEZZIWIG    (*laughing*) Ebenezer Scrooge! Do you hear me? Mr Scrooge! I request the pleasure! This instant!

(SCROOGE *makes a move towards her.*)

SCROOGE    Mrs Fezziwig! I am coming!

(*But* FAGIN *stops him, and he watches as his younger self downs his drink and runs to take his place as* MRS FEZZIWIG'S *partner in the next dance.*)

FAGIN    What a fine woman.

SCROOGE    I was devoted to her . . .

FAGIN    Did you know, she had two sons –

SCROOGE    What?

FAGIN    Who did not survive their infancy.

(SCROOGE *has no reply, just watches the dance.*)

FAGIN    She was so very fond of you.

SCROOGE    And I of her.

(*When the dance finishes, there is a scattering of applause,* MRS FEZZIWIG *speaks to* YOUNG SCROOGE.)

MRS FEZZIWIG    Mr Scrooge, you have been taking lessons without my knowledge! So handsome you are in your new scarf. At which point, my pet, you

say, and is that a new dress you're wearing
Mrs F – you look radiant, resplendent!

YOUNG
SCROOGE            Umm . . . Is that a new dress you're wearing,
Mrs F?

(*She laughs uproariously, smothers him in her
arms.*)

MRS FEZZIWIG   I love you Mr Scrooge, I really do! Let's see
about some cake, will we? Oh Lord, he's
clearing his throat. Quickly! Cake and a glass!
Cake and a glass!

(MR FEZZIWIG *stands on a chair.*)

FEZZIWIG           Good friends! Good friends. Every year on this
day, on Christmas Eve, I stand amazed at the
gifts you bring into our house. Your handsome
faces, your holiday finery, and your lightning
feet at the country dances – (*A cheer goes up.*)
And so it is, at this time of the long year, when
friends old and new, and precious family, all
come together to share a table, and celebrate
the simple things, and laugh about their
fortunes, and raise a glass to the yesterdays
gone by, and – oh dear – I'm crying again, as
usual – my wife will tease me something
shocking for this – oh dear me – carry on! –
it's a feast we have here, not a funeral!

(*Soppy old* FEZZIWIG *is led away, blowing his
nose. He is teased as he feared, and tickled till
he laughs.* MRS FEZZIWIG *starts up a chorus of
"For He's A Jolly Good Fellow".*)

FAGIN              Why do they love him so? He's not spent so
very much on them, after all?

SCROOGE           But don't you see – it's not about the *money,
man* –

Scene 10
The end of
the affair

(*The party breaks up, the music stops abruptly, the lights go all harsh.*)

What happened? Where are they — ? Why are they leaving?

FAGIN   They never left. You did. You wanted to "better" yourself. Trouble was, you thought "better" meant the same as "richer". And you became someone else. Here he is now. He has something to say to this lady. And she has something to say back, ~~I think~~. TO you

(*On a park bench sits* BELLE. EBENEZER, *"A man in the prime of life", is pacing by her.*)

EBENEZER   I don't know what you want from me. What you want me to say.

BELLE   And I don't know why you torture me so. Let me go.

EBENEZER   We have a contract.

BELLE   So then release me from it —

EBENEZER   Why should I —

BELLE   As I release you. Because that is what you want.

EBENEZER   (*mocking*) What I want.

BELLE   I have a rival, and she has me at a disadvantage —

EBENEZER   Belle, stop —

BELLE   Gold is your new love. She outshines me in every way, and if she can give you the happiness that I would wish for you, then I am content.

EBENEZER   Really, Belle — you're talking nonsense —

BELLE        Am I? Say – say this were the first time we
ever met. Do you think you would choose me
for your wife? Me – a plain girl from a poor
family? No, of course not –

EBENEZER    Belle – please, think about what you are
saying –

BELLE        I've thought about little else! And I release
you, Ebenezer.

SCROOGE     For heaven's sake –
EBENEZER
BELLE        For the love of him you once were. May you
be happy in the life you have chosen.

(BELLE *leaves him.* SCROOGE *fiddles with his
hat, head bowed. Then he dons it, and walks
off.*)

SCROOGE     Show me no more. Take me home, damn you!

FAGIN        Not yet.

SCROOGE     Why do you torment me!?

FAGIN        One more.

SCROOGE     No more, I say!

FAGIN        It's not for you to say, Young Gentleman.
(FAGIN *leads him to where a middle-aged man,*
RICHARD, *is playing a game with his* CHILDREN.
*This bit perhaps best worked out in rehearsal?
The game needs to be simple, so that it can be
actually played on stage, to give it that reality.
The voice of* BELLE *calls out from off, that she
is home. The* CHILDREN *run to greet her as she
enters.*)

BELLE        Halloo halloo! Happy Christmas Eve! Hello
you little rascals! Have they been good little
rascals?

RICHARD        Oh, very good – for the most part!

BELLE          Only the most part?

RICHARD        Well the game was very competitive, you
               know. Brings out the demon in a child, now
               and then. But never fear, all disputes have
               been kissed and made up.

BELLE          Disputes, ey? Sounds like fun . . .

RICHARD        It was!

BELLE          And now it's bedtime on Christmas Eve? All
               too much excitement, I might need a hug from
               one of my children . . . let's see, which one
               shall I have . . . I think it will have to be . . .
               BOTH of them!

FAGIN          (*watching* BELLE) Very sweet how the girls
               hang on to their mother like that. You know
               her, of course. The mother.

BELLE          Oh, lovely . . . Come on then Miss and Miss.
               Off you go to Bedfordshire – I'll be up in two
               shakes. Go go!

RICHARD        (*playfully*) And no rascally business up there –
               or I shall come and sing to you!

CHILDREN       Nooooo!!

BELLE          Now *there's* a threat!

               (*The* CHILDREN *exit, and* BELLE *and* RICHARD
               *embrace, they are very loving.*)

RICHARD        How are you?

BELLE          Oh I am extremely well, my boy.

SCROOGE        She does look well – and I am glad, glad she's –

| FAGIN | Say it. |
| SCROOGE | She's happy. |
| FAGIN | You're blushing. |
| SCROOGE | I am not! |
| FAGIN | So rarely are you in the presence of love. But listen to this. |
| RICHARD | I saw an old friend of yours in London. |
| BELLE | Who was that? |
| RICHARD | You'll never guess. |
| BELLE | (*laughing*) Then don't make me! Silly. |
| RICHARD | There he was in his office window, large as life. |
| BELLE | Was it Mr Scrooge? |
| RICHARD | It was indeed. |
| BELLE | How did he seem? |
| RICHARD | Miserable. |
| BELLE | Poor man. |
| RICHARD | All alone, by the light of one candle. And you know, his partner's on the point of death. |
| BELLE | Yes. |
| RICHARD | Quite alone in the world he'll be, I do believe it. |
| SCROOGE | Spirit, remove me from this place, at once! |
| FAGIN | Don't blame me. |

SCROOGE      Stop it!

FAGIN        But this is the way it was.

SCROOGE      Remove me! I'm begging you. I can't take any
             more of this! I can't look at any more! I won't!

             (SCROOGE *seizes* FAGIN's *lantern and brings it
             crashing down.*)

             (*Blackout.*)

## STAVE THREE
### The Second Of The Three Spirits

CHORUS *come tippy-toeing in, carrying candles. They form a
ring around* SCROOGE's *bed, which is slowly and softly
illuminated, and we see* SCROOGE *soundly asleep. And hear
him! He snores very loudly. The* CHORUS *might come and
tickle him, or lift up his limp limbs by way of demonstration.*

CHORUS       Ahh . . . !
             Sleepyhead
             Drowsy drawers
             Poor old Ebenezer
             Ebenezer Snooze
             He's knackered
             Exhausted
             Pooped
             Who wouldn't be
             After a haunting

             So awful
             A dream
             So vivid
             A lesson
             So hard . . .
             But no rest for the wicked.

             (*A bell sounds for One o'clock, very sharp,*
             SCROOGE *leaps out of bed terrified . . .* )

SCROOGE      YEAAH HAH! I'm ready for you, whatever
             you are! Come on now! Bring it! Bring it, I

say! Show yourself! You have to get up pretty
early to catch Me out, believe it! YAHAA!

CHORUS          Five minutes go by.

SCROOGE         Can't catch ME!

CHORUS          Ten.

                (SCROOGE *is ready.*)

SCROOGE         I'm ready!

CHORUS          For anything.
                Anything between a baby
                And a rhinoceros
                A baby rhinoceros, even
                The one thing
                He's not ready for
                Is
                Nothing.
                A quarter

                (*Bells.*)

                Of the hour
                No demon comes
                No shapeshifter
                No ghoul
                Or ghost
                Or spectre
                Not a sausage.
                (*A string of sausages appears with a splat.*
                SCROOGE *is astonished.*)

SCROOGE         What – in the name of all that's holy –

CHORUS          Spoke too soon.

                (SCROOGE *examines the string of sausages.*)

SCROOGE         Sausages – good quality – lamb, if I'm not
                very much mistaken –

(*Another splat.*)

Hey ho – plum pudding is it?

(*And another, and it starts raining food, and*
SCROOGE *goes about picking up item after item,
naming them –* "*turkeys, geese, game, brawn,
great joints of meat, sucking pigs, long
wreaths of sausages, mince-pies, plum-
puddings, barrels of oysters, red-hot chestnuts,
cherry-cheeked apples, juicy oranges, luscious
pears, immense twelfth- cakes*" *– with
increasing excitement and wonder, and as he
does so the* GHOST OF CHRISTMAS PRESENT *makes
his entrance, a strapping fellow in his prime,
attended by his* BAND OF FOLLOWERS, *all of
them making merry and accompanied by
stirring music. The* GHOST OF CHRISTMAS
PRESENT *steps forward and greets* SCROOGE *like
a long lost friend, throwing his arms around
him and giving him a bear-hug.* PRESENT'S
*attendants hand* SCROOGE *food and drink
during the following.* CHORUS *collect food.*)

PRESENT        Ebenezer, how very very VERY wonderful.
               Let me look at you. How the Dickens ARE
               you!?

SCROOGE        Do I know you?

PRESENT        Not yet you don't.

SCROOGE        Yet you presume to know me.

PRESENT        You *must* have met one of my brothers, surely.

SCROOGE        I don't believe so.

PRESENT        One of my sisters, then.

SCROOGE        Got a lot of siblings, have you?

PRESENT        More than eighteen hundred!

| | |
|---|---|
| SCROOGE | Eighteen hund – (*He gets it.*) I know who you are, you're – |
| PRESENT | (*offering him one*) Mince pie? |
| SCROOGE | (*taking it*) The second Spirit – The Ghost of Christmas Present! |
| PRESENT | (*bowing deeply*) Your servant. Come with me now. Don't be shy. And drink up, there. |
| SCROOGE | Where we going? |
| PRESENT | Drink up! I've so much to show you. |
| SCROOGE | Spirit, last night I was an unwilling pupil. And yet – I learned a thing or two. Take me where you will. |

(*There is a roll of thunder, and the space is cleared. Music. They are in the street, and it's freezing. During the following, the Cratchit house takes shape.*)

| | |
|---|---|
| CHORUS | The night |
| | The cold |
| | The soot |
| | The ice |
| | The snow |
| | The streets |
| | The people |
| | The air |
| | The breath |
| | The lights |
| | The fires |
| | The people |
| | The cheer |
| | The cheeks |
| | The games |
| | The laughs |
| | The still |
| | The quiet |
| | The place |

The house — *me*
~~The roof~~
The path
~~The door~~
The home
The hearth
The boys
The girls
~~The pride~~
The hopes — *me*
~~The heart~~
The fears
The love
The cares
The Cratchits. — *me*

PRESENT     Stay by my side.

SCROOGE     I will.

*save 15*
*a re cratch*

(*The* CRATCHITS *are preparing for Christmas dinner. *MRS C, BELINDA, *and* PETER *are getting the table ready in a hurry.* TIM *is watching for* BOB *at the window.* MARTHA *is bringing things in from the kitchen.* MRS C *will issue little instructions throughout.*)

SCROOGE     Who's he watching for?

PRESENT     You'll see.

BELINDA     It's cruel on Dad.

MARTHA      Oh Belinda.

BELINDA     It is.

PETER       No it's not.

MRS C       Bit of fun is all, she'll not let him stew, will you love.

MARTHA      Course I won't.

TIM          He's coming!

             (MARTHA *screams and scurries to hide under
             the table.* PETER *goes to look . . .* )

PETER        This is gonna be soooo funny. Hang on – I
             don't see him –

             (*He sees* TIM'S *cheeky smile.*)

             Oooh, you little devil!

TIM          (*laughing*) What's that on your face, Pete? It's
             EGG, I think! Ha ha!

MARTHA       (*re-emerging*) I'll swing for you, boy.

MRS C        See to the taters first, girl.

TIM          Got you! Ha ha ha!

MARTHA       (*to* TIM, *grudgingly fond*) Button it, you.
             Cheeky monkey.

MRS C        Oh – nuts!

             (TIM, MARTHA *and* PETER *burst out laughing.*)

TIM          Mind your language, will you Mum! It's
             Christmas!

MRS C        (*embarrassed but amused despite herself*)
             Don't be so crude. Just – I forgot them – your
             saying monkey reminded me –

TIM          Wait'll I tell Dad!

MRS C        Don't you dare!

             (*A hiatus of quiet as they each go about their
             business.*)

PRESENT      What d'you think of them, my friend.

SCROOGE    I think they are poor, and very fond of one
           another. (*Points at* TIM.) And isn't he a
           scream!

MRS C      Mind you behave when your father gets here.
           He works so very hard all year round –

TIM        (*kissing her*) We know, Mum – he's an angel
           sent from Heaven –

           (PETER *and* BELINDA *share a look and a smile.*)

MRS C      I don't know where you all learned to tease a
           person so, really I don't. Give that gravy a stir
           Tim, so it don't skin over.

TIM        Righty-ho . . .

MRS C      Pass him a spoon, someone. And no tasting!

           (*Too late –* TIM *has already had a mouthful,
           and cackles his delight.*)

SCROOGE    Greedy child!

PRESENT    Hungry child. And sickly.

SCROOGE    What is the matter?

PRESENT    His birth was hard, he and his mother barely
           survived it. Every penny went on medicines,
           doctors' fees. The pennies soon ran out. And
           so it began.

SCROOGE    What did?

PRESENT    Hardship and hunger.

SCROOGE    They starved?

PRESENT    Baby Tim was severely underweight. His
           development suffered. He suffers still. His
           limbs give him agony.

SCROOGE      But he's so lively!

PRESENT      And so very sick.

SCROOGE      Can you see his future? Will he get better?

             (*No answer.*)

             Cannot something be done?

PRESENT      As you say – they are a poor family.

TIM          Here he is!! Really this time! Quick Martha,
             quick!!

             (MARTHA *hides under the table,* MRS C *gets rid
             of her pinny,* PETER *checks everything is ready,*
             BELINDA *prepares a drink for her father, and
             all goes to generate a sense of an event.
             Briefest pause, everyone's ready, then* BOB
             *enters, carrying the goose on a platter.*)

BOB          TA-DAA!!

SCROOGE      Cratchit?! Bob Cratchit, my clerk . . .

             (*Everyone fusses round . . . shouting 'Hurray
             for the Goose!' and 'Happy Christmas
             Everyone', and squeezing and kissing* BOB.)

PRESENT      Does my heart good!! What about you, friend?

SCROOGE      It IS him –

BOB          But – but wait, wait – wherever is Martha??

             (*Short pause.*)

PETER        Jenny came by with a message from her.

BOB          What kind of a message?

MRS C        Not coming.

| | |
|---|---|
| BOB | Not coming? |
| PETER | (*carrying* TIM *to the table, where they both sit*) Mistress wouldn't let her off. |
| TIM | Too much work on, she said. |
| PETER | Big party, Boxing Day. |
| BOB | Not coming on Christmas dinner? Well. That's a blow, I must say – I've half a mind to go over there, you know and give them a piece of my mind! |

(MARTHA'S *hand has emerged from under the table and grabbed* BOB'S *ankle. He shrieks, which sets everyone laughing* . . . BOB *gets a kiss and a glass from* MRS C.)

| | |
|---|---|
| BOB | Devils, the lot of you! Tim put you up to it I bet? |
| TIM | Don't blame me! What have I ever done? |

(BOB *is behind him, ruffles his hair, squeezes his shoulders as he speaks.*)

| | |
|---|---|
| BOB | Everything's lovely, isn't it? All of us together. |
| TIM | The best Christmas yet, Dad. When I was going to sleep last night I was fed up cos it'll be over day after Boxing Day! Isn't that silly! |
| BOB | Very silly. |
| TIM | We mustn't worry about it being over, must we. |
| BOB | No, son. We mustn't. |
| TIM | Happy Christmas, Dad. |
| BOB | And many more to come, my boy. |

MRS C          Come on you two. Let's get this goose carved, will we?

               (*During the next exchange the Cratchits get themselves all seated and ready for dinner. With some dialogue between the Cratchits but under that of* SCROOGE *and* PRESENT, *this to be found in rehearsal, the minutiae of getting everything finally prepped.*)

PRESENT        Makes your mouth water, doesn't it.

SCROOGE        But – it's too small for such a family, surely –

PRESENT        It's what they can afford.

SCROOGE        Hardly a slice each!

PRESENT        There's mashed potato with it, and a carrot -

SCROOGE        Singular!

PRESENT        – and gravy, and apple sauce, and stuffing, and an orange to share.

               (*Time passes, and the dinner has gone down a treat.*)

TIM            So. Completely. Fantastic.

BOB            There's never been such a goose, love.

PETER          Heavenly.

SCROOGE        Look at the boy, licking his plate! Spirit – tell me – tell me he will live – you say he is very ill, like you know his case well – will he survive to see next Christmas, see another day like today?

               (PRESENT *gives him a look, then with great ceremony goes to the table, fills a glass and hands it to* BOB. *He does the same for himself and for* SCROOGE.)

BOB     A Merry Christmas to us all, my darlings. God bless us!

        (*General toasting and clinking of glasses, among which . . .*)

TIM     God bless us, every last one!

BOB     A toast. To Mr Scrooge – the founder of this feast.

MRS C   (*laughs contemptuously*) HA!     Song ) |

BOB     My dear.

MRS C   I'm sorry but I am not raising my glass to that man.

BOB     Dear – the children –

MRS C   The children! – why should you or I or any child of ours be grateful to that cruel, money-grabbing tyrant? What sort of example is he to anybody?

BOB     He gives me employment, and on this day of all days I think we should be glad of –

MRS C   Oh you do, do you. And when I was sick, and when our child is sick still –

BOB     Ellen –

MRS C   Sick, and suffers night and day for it –

BELINDA Mum –

MRS C   Not a penny spare for medicines –

PETER   Don't, Mum –

MRS C            – And if he should worsen –

                 (MRS C *is overcome, and gets up.*)

BOB              Come now, love – it's Christmas Day!

MRS C            I'm sorry!

                 (*She runs out of the room,* BELINDA *gets up and
                 follows.* BOB, TIM, PETER *and* MARTHA *sit in
                 silence.*)

SCROOGE          I can't bear it, Spirit – tell me the boy will live
                 to be a man.

PRESENT          Unless there is a change in their Fates, I see an
                 empty chair at their next Christmas feast.

                 (*The light fades.*)

SCROOGE          He will die . . .

PRESENT          THEN HE HAD BETTER DIE . . . (*This right
                 in* SCROOGE'S *face, in his own voice.*) . . . and
                 decrease the surplus population.

                 (*Interval.*)

## ACT TWO

Scene 1

*Mad Music, whirling and moaning, swooping and flying, and*
SCROOGE *and* PRESENT *are travelling at great speed, to a great*
*height*

Song 12

| | |
|---|---|
| CHORUS | The Ghost Of Christmas Present |
| | Seizes the breezes |
| | Whips the wind |
| | Clatters the clouds |
| | And they sweep |
| | And they soar |
| | Through the roaring night |
| | Over the land |
| | Till the land |
| | Is no more |
| | And all can be heard |
| | Is the churning |
| | And smashing |
| | Of the black black waves |
| | Beneath their flying feet |
| | |
| SCROOGE | Where are you taking me!!? |
| | |
| CHORUS | Scrooge is full |
| | Of Terror |
| | And Shame |
| | And Excitement |
| | All mixed together |
| | Holding on |
| | His mind a whirl |
| | He thought of Tim |
| | And himself |
| | And Tim again |
| | Their destinies |
| | Inseparable |
| | And he began |
| | To see |
| | The light |

Scene into light here

(*A Light, small at first then larger, larger, till*
*it's blinding . . . It sweeps across the field of*
*view, is gone, then comes back again . . . and*
*after its second swoop, two men are revealed,*

*sitting together quietly, playing cards and*
*drinking. Let's call them* ALF *and* WALLY. ALF
*looks at his pocket watch, puts it away. Brief*
*pause.*)

ALF            Hold up there, will you Wally.

WALLY          What for?

ALF            Handkerchief.

WALLY          What about it?

ALF            Other trousers.

WALLY          Oh.

               (ALF *gets up and fetches – not his hankie, but*
               *a book.*)

SCROOGE        What is this place?

PRESENT        Well let's see. It's a very high house . . . with
               a very large light on the top of it. And miles
               from any neighbour . . .

SCROOGE        Lighthouse keepers!

ALF            (*holding out a book to* WALLY) Here.

WALLY          What's that?

ALF            Christmas box.

WALLY          Is it midnight already, Alf?

               (ALF *nods,* WALLY *takes the book, opens it,*
               *looks at the title page.*)

ALF            Saw it in Chapel Market. It is Treasure Island,
               isn't it? The feller swore blind –

WALLY          Don't worry! Treasure Island it is.

ALF            You can read it out loud for me.

WALLY          I will. A present for us both. (WALLY *puts out
               his hand.*) Thanks.

               (ALF *takes it and they shake, warmly.*)

ALF            Happy Christmas, mate.

WALLY          Happy Christmas, Alf.

CHORUS         The Ghost of Christmas Present
               Blushed with pride
               To see the simple pleasure
               And strong affection
               Occasioned by
               His Christmas presence.

PRESENT        These men have hard lives, they live from
                    hand to mouth.
               But scratch them with holly thorns
               And there you see it
               The softness and benevolence within
               Fellow feeling
               Joy in friendship
               Respite from daily cares.
               I wish it so – for the whole world!!

               (*The Mad Travelling Music again, and the
               blinding sweeping light, and the journey in
               reverse. When they come to rest,* SCROOGE
               *begins to protest.*)

SCROOGE        Spirit, I am so weary – Take me home to my –
               I want to go to bed!

PRESENT        Bed? Pah. The night is young – and the game's
               afoot!

               (*A great shriek goes up, a playful scream, and
               we see . . .* FRED *and* BETTY *and their friends
               are playing blind-man's buff.*)

SCROOGE        It's Fred!

PRESENT        The very same. Your bright-eyed, big-hearted
               nephew, only child of your bright-eyed, big-
               hearted sister, whose early death still pains
               you, deep deep in your lonely heart. You deny
               it? Tell me – which one is Betty, his wife? You
               don't know? Ah, that's right, you declined
               their invitation to the wedding. You silly man.

               (*The game continues until* BETTY *and* FRED *end
               up in each other's arms, laughing.*)

FRED           Oh dear! I am not as young as I was!

BETTY          Nonsense – no excuses.

TOPPER         (*out of breath*) That was – that was a capital
               round – well played, Fan!

FAN            Thank you.

TOPPER         What shall we play now?

FRED           Mercy! I need a drink!

TOPPER         Christmas is not for the faint-hearted, my boy
               – up and at it!

BETTY          Let him breathe!

FAN            Bully boy!

TOPPER         Alright. His house, after all.

FAN            I know, Topper. Why don't we have a sitting
               down game.

BETTY          Yes!

TOPPER         Good notion that. A sitting down game.
               What'll it be?

| | |
|---|---|
| FRED | 'Yes and No'! |
| BETTY | 'Yes and No', of course. |
| FRED | (Who's first?) |
| TOPPER | You are. Fred is |
| FRED | Righto. How many questions? |
| FAN | Twenty. |
| FRED | Twenty. Good. Ahmmm . . . Got one. Fire away. |

(*And they do, taking not many questions to discover* FRED *is thinking of an animal. During the following* SCROOGE *might pitch in, and be told by* PRESENT *to save his breath, as they can't hear him.*)

| | |
|---|---|
| BETTY | Is it alive? |
| FRED | Yes. |
| TOPPER | Is it a dog? |
| FRED | NO! |
| FAN | Is it very savage? |
| FRED | Yes! |
| BETTY | That barks and growls? |
| FRED | Oh, yes. |
| FAN | Can you see it in town? |
| FRED | Yes. |
| TOPPER | Is it in a show? |
| FRED | No! |

BETTY          A zoo?

FRED           NO!

SCROOGE        It's a horse!

TOPPER         A pig.

FRED           No.

FAN            A bear.

FRED           No.

TOPPER         A cow?

FRED           NOOO!!!

               (FRED *is helpless with laughter at their
               bemusement.*)

TOPPER         We're no closer than when we started.

FAN            Damn you, sir!

BETTY          Is it a tiger?

FRED           Don't be silly.

TOPPER         A bullock!   is it human

FRED           No.

BETTY          An ass?

FRED           Now you're getting warmer!

FAN            (*jumping up, excited*) AH! I think I have it! I
               have it! Got you, Fred.

FRED           Go on then –

FAN            It's – your uncle SCROOOOOOOGE!!

(*Much merriment at this, and* SCROOGE *buries his face in his hands in horror.* FRED *goes and gets a refill and tops up everyone's glasses.*)

FRED    Uncle Ebenezer it is. And since he has given us all a good laugh, I think it only fair that we raise a glass to him, and drink his health. Come on all of you.

BETTY    Well, if we must!

FRED    I insist. To my dear uncle, I say. To Scrooge!

(*The company echo his toast, half-heartedly.*)

FRED    Well that's a damp squib of a toast if ever I heard one.

FAN    It's just – the name. That name

TOPPER    A bit of a dampener.

BETTY    Didn't he say to your face that Christmas was a humbug?

FRED    He's a comical old fellow, is all –

FAN    Comical?

FRED    It's my belief, he is to be pitied. His offences carry their own punishments, and I for one –

TOPPER    Rich feller like that's not to be pitied!

BETTY    I have no patience with him.

FRED    Well – I have. I couldn't be angry with him if I tried.

FAN    You're too good.

FRED    Nonsense. The only real consequence of his not being here and making merry with us, is

that he misses out. He's all alone on
Christmas, just like every other day. And I
think if ever a man is pitiable, it's for being
lonely, regardless if he himself is the cause of
that loneliness. I wish he were here with us
now, I really do –

TOPPER   If he thinks Christmas is all humbug, I'd
sooner he stayed where he is.

FRED   Topper my friend, I know you mean well to
this house but I can't agree. He may call
Christmas a humbug till he dies –

FAN   He may well –

FRED   – but he can't help thinking better of it – I
defy him – if year after year I look him in the
eye and say, "Uncle – how are you?" If it only
puts him in the vein to be a little kinder to his
clerk by and by, leave him fifty pounds in his
will, perhaps – (*They laugh at the idea.*) – Go
on and laugh, but I really think I got through
to him yesterday –

TOPPER   Oh, dear!

FAN   Dear Fred!

BETTY   Such a sentimental fish –

TOPPER   Another drink! We'll toast your uncle's health,
just to please you, and then – well we really
must be getting on.

FAN   Time to go carolling!

BETTY   Yes!!

TOPPER   That's settled. One for the road –

(*Glasses are charged.*)

To Uncle Scrooge!

*him*

FRED    A Merry Christmas to ~~the old man~~, and a
        Happy New Year.

ALL     Uncle Scrooge!

FRED    May God bless him.

SCROOGE And you, dear Fred! And you!

*Scene 5
in the
alleys of
despair*

        (*The party starts to leave, singing "Oh come
        all ye faithful, joyful and triumphant . . ."*)

        Can we follow?

PRESENT They are vanished to us. And my time is
        running out.

SCROOGE How so?

PRESENT I die at midnight.

SCROOGE Are spirits' lives so short?

PRESENT My life upon this earth is very brief. Come.

SCROOGE Where are we going.

PRESENT Home.

SCROOGE Home. What is that. Home to my self-willed
        prison cell.

        (*An ominous air, unsettling sounds. It's dark,
        they have to pick their way through it.*)

PRESENT Stay close.

SCROOGE I'm frightened, Spirit.

PRESENT I am here.

SCROOGE What is this place?

PRESENT      Your neighbourhood.

SCROOGE      Really?

PRESENT      The streets you choose to avoid. The paths you have never walked.

SCROOGE      Why do you bring me here?

PRESENT      Look. *Song 14*

(TWO CHILDREN *are emerging from the gloom.*)

SCROOGE      What are they?

PRESENT      Children, that live in this gloom, they sleep in the filth behind the wall yonder.

SCROOGE      Where are their parents?

PRESENT      One is dead, from the cholera two years since. The other in prison. What does it matter?

SCROOGE      It matters to them!

(*The* CHILDREN *are close now.*)

PRESENT      Look at this boy. What do you see in his face?

SCROOGE      I'm sure – I'm sure he is a good boy –

PRESENT      Look at him. He has no self-worth. No understanding. No empathy. No, he is not good. Say your name, boy.

BOY      Ignorance.

PRESENT      Louder.

BOY      Ignorance!

PRESENT      See, his sister is too weak to stand. Speak for her, boy. Say her name.

| | |
|---|---|
| Boy | Poverty! |

(PRESENT *picks up the girl, takes the boy by the hand.*)

PRESENT    Poverty. And Ignorance. Starved, wild, lost. What do you suppose will happen to them when I am gone?

SCROOGE    I suppose they will remain as they are –

PRESENT    These children are the disgrace of this society, the shameful secret of the affluent, a stain on them that call themselves the *better sort* – for shame. A thousand like these, ten thousand more, skulking and cowering –

(PRESENT *turns away, leading the children.*)

SCROOGE    Spirit? But – Have they nowhere to go – no refuge or means of relief – ?

PRESENT    (*turning to glower at him*) Are there no prisons? Are there no WORKHOUSES?

(SCROOGE *sinks to his knees. Bells begin tolling for Midnight.*)

## STAVE FOUR
The Last Of The Three Spirits

*As the last bell's vibrations fade, the giant figure of* DEATH, *aka* THE GHOST OF CHRISTMAS YET TO COME, *has appeared, and moves toward* SCROOGE.

SCROOGE    Are you – are you the Ghost of Christmas Yet To Come? You are about to show me the shadows of things that have not yet happened? I fear you more than any spectre I have seen tonight. But as I know you mean to do me good – and as I hope to be a better man – I welcome you, truly I do – but oh! – you are fearsome!

(*Nothing from* DEATH.)

Will you not speak? Tell me what you are, and
what you will do!

(*Nothing. Instead, the scene shifts, and we are
in the business quarter of town, and men in
frock coats raising their hats to each other as
they go briskly about their business, and a
general air of busy-ness. Two men stop and
chat . . .*)

KING            Good morning, Mr Falkner.

FALKNER         Mister King. How are you?

KING            Well, thank you, very well –

FALKNER         Ready for a holiday?

KING            Christmas again.

FALKNER         Life is repetitive, if nothing else!

KING            See old Scratch kicked the bucket, ey?

FALKNER         So I hear . . . Damned cold, isn't it?

KING            The season for it, I suppose! . . .

SCROOGE         Spirit – What does this mean? I am acquainted
                with these men – but they never had any great
                importance for me or my affairs –

                (*Still nothing from* DEATH.)

                They say someone has passed away – but who?
                They can't mean Jacob, since he died in the
                Past, of course –

                (*Nothing.*)

I must watch and see for the reason, for reason
there must surely be, I know you spirits by
now.

KING    I only just heard from Giles, when they called
round to see about the contract –

FALKNER    I thought he was indestructible.

KING    Well there you are.

FALKNER    What's he done with his money, I wonder.

KING    Hasn't left it to *me*, that's for certain!

(*They both laugh a little laugh.*)

FALKNER    Likely to be a cheap funeral.

KING    Yes . . . You think anyone'll show up?

FALKNER    There's a thought.

KING    Suppose we make up a party, volunteer.

FALKNER    I don't know.

KING    If there's a lunch?

FALKNER    If there's a lunch . . .

KING    We'll see if there's a lunch.

(*And they go.*)

SCROOGE    So some poor fellow has weighed anchor, and
set sail toward that dark horizon. But who?
You are riddling with me, Spirit. I am positive
you mean me well – in spite of your, your –
You'll forgive me, but you are truly
frightening to look upon – and the silence –
the quite of the grave! – it would so chill me if
I did not feel –

(*A rumbling sound, and* DEATH *advances towards him slowly, and the sounds become threatening, menacing . . .* )

SCROOGE     Spirit, no . . . I beg you! Come no closer. Stay away! Mercy! MERCY!

(*A ghostly crescendo,* SCROOGE *falls to the ground . . . When he opens his eyes, as the noise abates, he sees* SAIREY *staring down at him, laughing.* SAIREY *is a mid-wife, and layer-out of corpses. She's dressed in a raggedy pinny, with bloodstains on the front.*)

*Scene 9*

*meeting with a midwife*

SAIREY     Oh dear, oh dear, look at the state of ya, Mister Ebenezer sir. You've gone pale as a muffin, you 'ave.

SCROOGE     Who the blazes are you?

SAIREY     I'm the midwife.

SCROOGE     Midwife?

SAIREY     I've brung out three this evenin', three little pink blobs, same birthday as our Saviour.

SCROOGE     What are you talking about?

SAIREY     It's Christmas, ain't it! They been sprung from the traps on Christmas. Whaddayer say about that?

SCROOGE     Leave me alone.

SAIREY     But sir, I've come – I'm here to, as you like to put it, help you up the ladder to salivation.

SCROOGE     I beg your pardon.

SAIREY     Help you on your way, you know.

SCROOGE     My way? To where?

SAIREY     Well that's not for the like of me to judge, I'm
           only the bringer-in and the general
           whatjamacallit, inn I? Tell you this for free, as
           well. There's an amount of gin in me besides – !

SCROOGE    I can smell it on you.

SAIREY     I wet the babies' heads, dun I. Very important
           tradition. When I'm at me other trade, the
           drinkin's even more partook.

SCROOGE    Oh? What trade is that, pray tell.

SAIREY     A layer-out, sir, is the other string to my
           fiddle.

SCROOGE    Layer-out – of what?

SAIREY     Of corpses, o' course. Come wi' me, I'll show
           you. Don't worry your old bonce, Mr Ebenezer
           – the fog'll clear in a minute, really it will, and
           you'll see –

           *Scene 10*

           *laying out
           of the dead*

           (SAIREY *leads* SCROOGE *to a gloomy space,
           where a body is laid out.* SCROOGE *gets only so
           far before the stench beats him back.* SAIREY
           *carries on, and busies herself taking the shirt
           off the dead body.*)

SCROOGE    Oh! God! The smell! How can you bear it?

           (*While she talks,* SAIREY *puts the shirt on top
           of a pile of other garments. She takes a flannel
           and gives the body a quick once-over. But*
           SCROOGE *never sees the face. She takes a small
           bottle of ointment, pours some on her hands
           and rubs it on the body. But carelessly. When
           she's finished she throws a shroud over the
           body, including the face.*)

SAIREY     The special pleasure in this work is to catch
           the ones without family, you know, the
           spinsters and the whatsits, the bachelors.
           Assuringly, the ones without family, they're

the prize begonias, tellin' yer. Ones with
widders, mind, and with 'alf a million children
all a-screechin' and a-moanin', the reg'lar
kind, I'd rather leave 'em than take 'em, truth
be told, but creeturs like me, we can't never
turn our noses up at a brass farthing. No
indeed. This is my lot, my calling, and so it
must be my pleasure.

SCROOGE    But surely, if there's no family to pay you – ?

SAIREY     Undertaker coughs up. He don't want to be
laying out. He's got other fish to fry, inn he.
He leaves me to fend and forage for meself,
and so I do. Me own fishy business. A cod and
a winkle. (*She picks up the bundle of clothes.*)
That's us. We're off.

SCROOGE    Where?

SAIREY     Sell this little lot, before Joe closes up.

SCROOGE    What? Sell the clothes off his back!

SAIREY     Ain't you been listening?

SCROOGE    This is how you – ? This is your living? It's
disgusting.

SAIREY     What's the point a buryin' a fine bit of stuff
like these? I'll bring him a calico shirt, he'll
be decent enough when he meets his Maker.
Don't you look down at me, Mister 'Eavy
Sneezer. It's a job. And as I say, a bachelor's a
prize (*begonia*) –

SCROOGE    Begonia, yes, as you say. But look at him.
What was he, I wonder –

SAIREY     Naught to any one. Years on his ownsome,
bitter as a barrel o' salt. Drove away his only
living blood. Rich but only in money. Treated

other people worse than dogs, an exploiter, a squeezer —

SCROOGE     Oh God.

SAIREY      — a curse-ed money-lender.

SCROOGE     Who are you?

SAIREY      You're shaking, Mr Squeezer.

SCROOGE     Show me the face.

SAIREY      You've seen some sights tonight, my dove —
            I'm not sure you can undertake it —

SCROOGE     Show me!

            (*She pulls back the cloth.*)

SAIREY      Ebenezer Scrooge, look into my black eyes —
            Look! Now you know me. This is you. In my
            power. Your Christmas Future.

SCROOGE     No. No, Spirit — it isn't so! This is surely a
            nightmare!

SAIREY      I'm not no blot of mustard, or crumb of
            cheese. Be sure of that.

            (*The* CHORUS *remove the body.*)

SCROOGE     But I cannot die, not now! Not when I have
            begun to see — for the first time in my life!
            There is so much for me to do!

            (*Street scene (at Xmas time of course) and
            here comes* FRED, *bustling along. He passes*
            BOB, *who is walking dolefully, head down.*
            FRED *doubletakes, remembers, calls after* BOB.)

FRED        I say there! Hello! Just a minute!

(BOB *doesn't hear,* FRED *has to go running after him and tap him on the shoulder.*)

FRED      Begging your pardon –

BOB       What – oh. Can I help you at all sir?

FRED      Is it – ? Dear me, I'm quite embarrassed – I don't know your name but –

BOB       Take your time, sir.

FRED      Thank you! – the thing is – damn it! (*He puts out his hand.*) The name's Fred. And if I'm not mistaken –

BOB       (*shaking his hand*) Mr Scrooge's nephew. I remember you now, sir.

FRED      And I you!

BOB       My sincere – my condolences to you and all the family sir.

FRED      Thank you very much. And how do you do these days – umm –

BOB       It's Bob, sir. Bob Cratchit.

FRED      Bob. Of course. Mr Cratchit. Look – I hope you don't mind me asking this – only, when I saw you, I was struck –

BOB       Don't worry yourself, sir. Ask away.

FRED      You looked so – I wonder, have you been able to find yourself a new situation?

BOB       Ah well, yes and no, sir. Bits and pieces.

FRED      I see. It's not easy, ey.

BOB       Life's a battle and it must be fought . . . I read that somewhere.

| | |
|---|---|
| FRED | Quite so. Very true. But now – are you sure there's nothing the matter? |
| BOB | Well sir – truth be told I've just come back visiting my son, Tim. |
| FRED | Oh really, and where is *he*? |
| BOB | In the cemetery, sir. St Martin's. |
| FRED | Mr Cratchit, I am so sorry – |
| BOB | Thank you, sir. |
| FRED | What a terrible blow for you, your poor wife – When did it happen? Dear man – no wonder you – |
| BOB | Three weeks it'll be, tomorrow. He was all determined to see the Christmas, but he didn't say much on the Saturday which was very unlike him, being a chatty sort of boy, you know, then when he went to bed on the Sunday – |

(BOB *crumples and throws himself into* FRED'S *arms.* FRED *leads him away.*)

| | |
|---|---|
| SAIREY | Behold. Your legacy. |

(*The scene is once again the Cratchits' house. There's a very different mood in the place.* MRS C *is working at some stitching.* PETER *is reading.* MARTHA *is drinking tea.* MRS C *gets up for a stretch, rubs her eyes.*)

| | |
|---|---|
| MARTHA | You look tired, ma. |
| MRS C | Hmm? |
| BELINDA | Go up for a nap. |
| MRS C | Oh no. It's just my eyes. How's the book? |
| BELINDA | I suppose it's alright. Exciting, and that. |

| | |
|---|---|
| MARTHA | Will I pour you a cup, after all? |
| MRS C | I'll wait till your father – ah! |
| BELINDA | Timing. |
| MRS C | Speak of the devil, and he comes. |

(BOB *enters, and there are muted hellos, and kisses.*)

| | |
|---|---|
| MRS C | Cold is it? |
| BOB | I'll say. |
| MRS C | Martha's just getting the tea. |
| BOB | Oh good. |
| BELINDA | Here, let me warm your hands. |
| BOB | Thanks. |
| MRS C | Nice, was it. |
| BOB | Oh, very. As the sun was setting it was on the frost, you know, and the mist rolling around the place – very pretty it was, and very calm. |
| MRS C | I'll go with you tomorrow. |
| BELINDA | We're all going, aren't we? |
| MRS C | Aye. Peter too. |
| BOB | Well that'll be nice, I must say. |

(*Pause.*)

| | |
|---|---|
| SCROOGE | Such pain they're in! And the poor boy! Poor Tim! Tell me – I have to know – |

| | |
|---|---|
| SAIREY | You want to know if this is fixed. If the future can be different. |
| SCROOGE | If I may be spared, to change my life – to change this future! – I am not the man I was! |

(SAIREY *puts her finger to her lips.*)

| | |
|---|---|
| BOB | Lovely glass of porter it was, and he says to me, Mr Cratchit – and he has the pleasantest voice on him, mind – Mr Cratchit he says, I am heartily sorry for it, and heartily sorry for your good wife. How he ever knew *that*, I *don't* know, by the way. |
| MRS C | Knew what? |
| BOB | That you were a good wife. |
| MRS C | Don't be cheeky. |
| BELINDA | Everybody knows that! |
| BOB | I should hope they do. Anyway there's his card, and he said if he could ever be of service to us in any way, I should be sure to call on him. |
| MRS C | Bless me, and him a blood relative of Scrooge's, too. |
| MARTHA | Wonders never cease. |
| BOB | We won't speak ill of the dead. But I had the feeling – there was something – in the earnest way he looked at me – |
| MRS C | What is it? |
| BOB | It was as if – as if he wanted to make amends. Like he had a heavy heart from knowing we'd never had much – much in the way of kindness from his uncle while he lived. |
| MRS C | I'm sure he is a good soul. |

| | |
|---|---|
| MARTHA | Drink your tea, Papa. |
| BOB | Alright my love. I was just thinking, it's only a pity our Tim – |
| PETER | Go on, Dad. |
| BOB | It was a pity he never met old Scrooge. He was always so frosty – It may be – sure our Tim could've warmed him up a little. |

(MARTHA *comes to kiss her father, and the light fades on the Cratchits.*)

| | |
|---|---|
| SCROOGE | But he did! He has! He has thawed me completely! Oh Spirit of the Future – let me live again, give me life, and I will USE it! |
| SAIREY | Look! |

*Scene 13, in the graveyard of the future* [handwritten]

(*The* CHORUS *are bringing on a massive headstone bearing his name.*)

No one ever escapes me. No one!

| | |
|---|---|
| SCROOGE | Good Spirit – why do you show me the Future, if not to grant me a place in it? A chance in it? Tell me it is not too late! Tell me I can change these shadows! I will honour – I promise it! – I will honour Christmas in my heart, and in my actions, and I will keep it all the year! I will live in the Past, the Present and the Future. The Spirits of all three shall live within me! I will take to my wounded heart the lessons they teach! Oh tell me I may wipe away the writing on this stone! |

*Scene 14* [handwritten]

*The rebirth of scrooge* [handwritten]

### STAVE FIVE
The End Of It

SCROOGE *wakes, sobbing. Then it hits him. He leaps out of bed.*

SCROOGE        I'm here. Still here. Am I really here? I – am.
               Somebody pinch me. I'm light as a feather.
               How long was I with the Spirits? I don't know.
               I don't know anything. I'm like a newborn
               baby. She was a midwife too, that laid out my
               dead body! Yes. Wonderful. And Fagin was
               there, and the Spirit of Christmas Present – all
               three came bearing gifts, like the Kings come
               to see the babe in the manger! I thought I was
               dead, but I wasn't! I was just being born! By
               the Spirits, and by the sad old shade of Jacob
               Marley – Thank you Jacob! – I will begin my
               life again. Starting when? I'll show you when.

               (*He strides over to the window, throws it open,
               shouts.*)

               Boy!

INTELLIGENT
BOY            Me sir?

SCROOGE        Yes you, sir! What day is it?

BOY            You what? You joking?

SCROOGE        Oh, he's a fine boy – Would you be so good –
               What day is today?

BOY            (*aside*) We've got a right one, here . . . It's
               CHRISTMAS DAY!

SCROOGE        Christmas Day! Wait there, boy! There's a
               shilling in it for you!
               (SCROOGE *goes to find something to write on,
               the* CHORUS *supply him.*)

               The Spirits have done it all in one night! They
               can do anything they like, of course they can –
               Ah, thank you – Of course they can!

               (*Back to the window.*)

               Halloo! My fine fellow!

| | |
|---|---|
| BOY | Hello? |
| SCROOGE | You know the butcher's in Tavistock Street? |
| BOY | (*rubbing his tummy*) Ooh yes. Mmmm. Know it well. |
| SCROOGE | An intelligent boy! A remarkable boy, don't you think so? |

(*The* CHORUS *chorus their agreement, cheerfully.*)

Do you know if they've sold the turkey that was hanging in the window?

| | |
|---|---|
| BOY | What – the massive one as big as me? |
| SCROOGE | A delightful boy, it's a pleasure to talk to him! Yes, my friend, the big one! |
| BOY | Nah, still there – |
| SCROOGE | Go and buy it. |
| BOY | (*calling to the street*) Copp – ER!! |
| SCROOGE | I am quite serious – here are my instructions – the bird to be sent to this address, and the bill to me! Come back with the receipt and I'll give you a shilling – no – two shillings – no – half a crown! |

(BOY *shoots off, delighted at the exchange.*)

It'll be on its way to Bob Cratchit's very soon! He won't know it's from me.

(SCROOGE *sets about dressing, with the* CHORUS'S *help.*)

| | |
|---|---|
| CHORUS | The sun is dawning<br>The light is pouring |

Through the damp
And the dark
Recesses of
His rusted heart.
His face a picture
Dazed and amazed
His voice a fountain
Of gurgling
And giggling
And chuckling sounds
Come bubbling up.
See Ebenezer
Quaking
Making resolutions
Bracing himself
Getting dressed
Ready and raring
Steeling himself
Like a baby
Learning to walk
Rehearsing his steps
Best foot forward
Into the garden of the world
For the first time.

(*A stream of people walking up and down, and*
SCROOGE *among them. People wish him Merry*
*Christmas, and he returns the compliment . . .*)

SCROOGE     A strange new world – look! there's a smile on
my face – incredible – I send it on its way, and
it comes back to me redoubled – !

(*He spots* MISS LEMON. *At once he wants to*
*make amends, but passes her two or three*
*times before plucking up the courage . . .*)

That is the charitable woman I sent packing
from my chambers! Ghost of Christmas
Present, I pray you can see what I am about to
do, and support me now, for it is no easy thing
for an Ebenezer Scrooge! Such as he was –

(*He goes up to* MISS LEMON.)

SCROOGE      My dear lady – how do you do?

MISS LEMON   Good God! Mr Scrooge –

SCROOGE      It is very excellent work you do. May I wish
             you a very Merry Christmas.

MISS LEMON   Is it? Pardon me, sir – are you Mr Scrooge?

SCROOGE      Yes – and no. That is my name, and I fear it
             may not be pleasant to you. Allow me to ask
             your forgiveness. And will you be good
             enough to come again and see me in my office,
             I wish to make a small donation –

             (*Here* SCROOGE *comes close to* MISS LEMON, *to
             whisper in her ear.* MISS LEMON *is shocked.*)

MISS LEMON   Good Lord! My dear Mr Scrooge! Are you
             serious?

SCROOGE      Not a penny less. A great many back payments
             are included in it, believe me. Will you come
             and see me?

MISS LEMON   My dear sir! Sir – of course I will.

SCROOGE      I look forward to it. And thank you, fifty
             times.

             (*They shake hands, with feeling.* MISS LEMON
             *goes.*)

CHORUS       Ebenezer turned
             And turned again
             And everywhere
             In the rattling cabs
             In the church steeples
             In the passing faces
             Ruddy with cold
             He saw it
             The beauty of the world
             Unfolding

Unfurling
Like a flower in wintertime
Unexpected joy

(CHORUS *sing "Oh come all ye faithful, joyful and triumphant . . . Bethlehem." * SCROOGE *has made his way to* FRED'S *house. He calms himself, girds himself, and knocks at the door.* FRED'S *housemaid answers.*)

LUCY           Good evening.

SCROOGE        Good evening to you, and a Merry Christmas.

LUCY           Oh, the same to you, sir.

SCROOGE        Is your master at home?

LUCY           I'm afraid he's out, sir.

SCROOGE        Oh.

LUCY           But he will be back shortly, for supper.

SCROOGE        He will?

LUCY           He's gone out carol-singing with the mistress, and their guests.

SCROOGE        Of course he has! Of course.

LUCY           Would you like to wait for him, sir?

SCROOGE        Do you know – I think I would.

               (SCROOGE *and* LUCY *enter the house, she takes his coat and hat, and she shows him to a seat.*)

LUCY           What name will I tell him, sir? When he comes back.

SCROOGE        Tell him – Simply tell him, his mother's brother has come to visit.

LUCY            (*surprised*) I will, sir –

                (*She goes, and the* CHORUS *sing the first verse
                of the concluding Carol. The restorative power
                of love, the gentler side of human nature,
                compassion and forgiveness – The pleasures
                of benevolence. During which . . .* FRED *enters
                at a run, clocks* SCROOGE. SCROOGE *gets up, and
                without a word they come together and
                embrace.*)

CHORUS          Next morning
                Worse the wear
                For all the games
                And dances
                And glasses of iced champagne
                Ebenezer Scrooge –
                Same name,
                Different man –
                Lay in wait
                For his prey
                Who was wonderfully late

                (SCROOGE *is in his office.*)

SCROOGE         Eighteen minutes! Eighteen minutes and a half
                – late! This is delicious!

                (SCROOGE *hears* BOB *approach, picks up a
                poker, giggles to himself.*)

                No! Must be stern. Straight face . . .

                (BOB *comes skidding in, off with his coat, hat
                and scarf, leaps into his chair* . . . )

SCROOGE         WHAT do you think you're doing coming in at
                this time of day?!

BOB             Very sorry for it, sir –

SCROOGE         Nineteen minutes!

BOB             I didn't mean to be late, sir –

| | |
|---|---|
| SCROOGE | (*wielding the poker*) Come here. If you please. |
| BOB | It won't happen again sir – I'm afraid I was making rather merry with my family – it's only once a year sir – . . . |
| SCROOGE | Come here. |

(BOB *gets up, terrified, and goes to* SCROOGE.)

| | |
|---|---|
| | Now. I am NOT going to stand for this sort of thing, Cratchit. Do you HEAR me? |
| BOB | No sir. I mean, yes, sir. |
| SCROOGE | And therefore. Do you know what I am going to do? Bet you can't guess. |
| BOB | Please sir – |
| SCROOGE | I am going to give you – . . . |
| BOB | Don't sir, please – |
| SCROOGE | A PAY RISE! |
| BOB | Sir? |

(*During the following, the* CHORUS *come to watch, and the principal* (*living*) *players* – FRED *and* BETTY, MISS LEMON, MRS C, TIM *and the other* CRATCHITS.)

| | |
|---|---|
| SCROOGE | Don't look at me like that, man, I'm quite well. Never better, in point of fact. A Merry Christmas to you, Bob. And a happier and more prosperous New Year, I hope. And how is the family, mm? Look here. I want you to tell me all about them. Your children – how are they doing? Wait! Make up the fires, put the kettle on while you're about it. We'll warm up, and then you will tell me all your affairs, |

all the ins and outs. You have a son I believe —
Tim? Who has not been in the best of health?

BOB           I do, sir, yes —

SCROOGE       But the fires first, and some tea! Then we'll
              see about a doctor for Tim, yes. But tea first,
              Mr Cratchit! Lovely tea! Or . . . or is it too
              early for some rum punch? What do you say,
              Bob?

BOB           Yes, sir! That would be — very welcome.

SCROOGE       Then let's have some! Hair of the dog that bit
              us, ey Bob!

BOB           Rum punch coming up sir! Right away!

              (*The* CHORUS *serve them punch, and everyone
              has a glass, as they sing a toast to the
              resurrection of Ebenezer, and bring this ghost
              story to its end.*)

                         SONG

              Raise your glasses;
              We will have a toast
              To the memory
              Of Marley's ghost,
              Marley's ghost.

              He gave Ebenezer
              A Christmas present,
              The chance to breathe again.
              A life changing lesson.

              So cheers Ebenezer,
              We're all here to say
              "Happy new life this Christmas
              And returns of the day".
              Many returns of the day.

              (*The End.*)

Mr Crummels — Joel
Mrs Crummels — Sabrina
Mr Folair — Lisa
Mrs snevalechi — Erica
Infant Phenomenon — Venky
Mr lenvil — Jay
Miss lenvil — Tressa

Notes. Crummels get in a group.
        Semi circle band Scrooge
come down on the sack

Bob's journey home

Screen / during fam & back

Marley's entrance

Streets of London

Death

X-mas present

Allys of despair

HANG ON TO ENERGY
IN EACH SCENE

Attack more with
the language

Keep the chimp for
Scrooge

look out occasionally
when controlly stuff

Dress run 1 FEEDBACK.

VOCAL ENERGY UP ↑ MAX

write down what you do.

GET IT OUT!

Work together. Avoid blame Culture

Adjust don't make a line

Be bigger crummels dont be too
sharp.

---

Dress run 2. Notes.

be lighter with the foothel

Go on the bells